Fruitful Droppings

D0318258

ISBN 1 869 822 70 6
First published 1997 by Pathway Books
Distributed by Subud Publications International Ltd.
Loudwater Farm, Loudwater Lane, Rickmansworth,
Herts WD3 4HG, UK

Cover design by Dirk Campbell
Typesetting by Leonard Hurd
Printed by The Book Factory, London

Fruitful Droppings

from the legacy of
VARINDRA TARZIE VITTACHI
Communicator of Genius

1921 – 1993

A SHORT SELECTION
from his sayings, talks, articles,
public addresses and papers
for the United Nations

Compiled and edited by Matthew Barry Sullivan

pathway

Other books by
Varindra Tarzie Vittachi

Emergency '58 –
The Story of the Ceylon Race Riots, Deutsch, 1958

The Island in the Sun, A.N.C. Colombo, 1960

The Brown Sahib, Deutsch, 1962

The Fall of Sukarno, Deutsch, 1967

The Brown Sahib Revisited, Penguin, 1987

Between the Guns – Children as a Zone of Peace,
Hodder and Stoughton, 1993

A Special Assignment – A Subud Trilogy,
Subud Publications International, 1996

A Life in Brief

'Communicator of genius and nobility' ran the headline of the *Guardian* obituary when Varindra Tarzie Vittachi died near Oxford on September 18th, 1993. At the age of thirty-two he became editor of the *Ceylon Observer*, the oldest English language paper in Asia and dedicated himself, at the risk of assassination, to exposing folly and pomposity, tyranny and man's inhumanity to man. Most unusually he was also deeply interested in the inner processes of the mind and emotions. Already as a boy he was asking the big questions – the why and wherefore of existence.

He was born, the eldest of thirteen children at Pillikiathuwa near Gampala, north of Colombo. His Buddhist father, the village school master, named him Abhaya (fearless) Gamini, but his agility among the trees in the neighbouring forest soon earned him the nickname Tarzan, which was quickly abbreviated to Tarzie. The agility and exuberance of his tongue was no less remarkable. It is told that between lessons at Ananada College a corridor might well be blocked by boys crowding round him, captivated by his story-telling. Later on, his stories, whether true or invented, hilarious or mischievous, became like a personal passport. He discovered that this was how to make people listen to him or read him on serious matters, and in journalism conveyed more of the truth than mere facts. Both feared and fearless, he made the *Observer* a forum for debating great issues. But it is by the nom-de-plume Flybynight that he is chiefly remembered in Sri Lanka to this day.

With playful effrontery he invented an 'Island in the Sun' inhabited by a huge cast of animal politicians, who each week played out their power-games, with identifiable style and gusto. He lampooned the new class of 'Brown Sahibs' (a term he is credited with inventing) who imitated their former masters. His fame as a laughter-maker was such that citizens would be seen lining up outside his bungalow to be photographed beside the house of Flybynight, scourge of politicians.

When in 1954 the young James Grant came as head of US AID to Sri Lanka the US ambassador warned him against Tarzie as a firebrand. The tall, strongly Christian American with a benevolent sharp-cut face and the Buddhist-born 'small brown bundle of energy' soon became close friends. They both had a similar vision of the post-colonial world, and sensed a coming revolution in human awareness that would give ordinary people a voice in their affairs. Grant judged the island to be 'earmarked for an experiment in democracy which had already begun before independence', with Tarzie as its most powerful defender.

But the experiment was nearly over. In 1956 a nationalist government, vociferously backed by militant Buddhists, swept into power through their chauvinist slogan 'Sinhala Only', creating a unitary state and so driving the Tamils into a corner. As Tarzie accurately forecast, this four-letter word 'Only' led to a racial bloodbath. The press was muzzled and Tarzie escaped into exile in 1961.

Subud

Tarzie's rejection of religion as he saw it in practice and his search for inner truth at first led him into an esoteric way, the self-study system of Gurdjieff. But 1957 brought him into the circle of Subud, a new spiritual movement which offers contact, by a method of self-surrender, with the Power of God, or the Great Life Force. It gives those who are 'opened' in Subud access to the common source of all the great religions. Through a spiritual exercise known as the *latihan* members are enabled to become inwardly cleaner and to grow into their potential as human beings.

Tarzie decided to investigate the truth of this for himself. He, the hard-nosed journalist and arch Doubting Thomas, found something so real, so subtle, so intelligent and undeniable, that he joined, committing himself to its founder, Muhammad Subuh, as his guide and mentor. Before long he became one of Pak Subuh's most trusted spokesman and roving ambassadors, and in 1963 was made chairman of the International Subud Brotherhood (later Association), a position he held almost until his death. He also received and added to his own the extra name of Varindra, by which he is known throughout the tiny but world-wide Subud community.

The second stage of Tarzie's life was devoted to bringing about a revival of Asian consciousness, after centuries during which all the strings of power had led back to western capitals. He first worked for the International Press Institute, infusing a whole generation of Asian journalists with his ideals of a responsible press in post-colonial societies, aided by a technical assistance programme. He co-founded with the brilliant Bengali journalist Amithaba Chowdhury the independent Press Foundation of Asia, based in Manila, which organised two remarkable All Asia Assemblies, the first of their kind. With Chowdhury too he created 'Development Journalism', which was able mostly to avoid censorship by being neither pro- nor anti-government, but pro-people. Its high aim was to 'write the diary of the new nation, as it struggles to conquer poverty and establish a new sense of dignity for the common man'.

In 1971 in Hong Kong with a few friends, finance from

the Philippines and expert assistance from the London *Times*, Tarzie set up and brilliantly edited the first regional newspaper in the world, *The Asian*. This time he significantly chose as his pseudonym the name of Arjuna, the archer and charioteer in the Hindu epic Bhagavad Gita , who is shown how he can follow a spiritual path although engaged in the bloodiest heat of the battle. Every Sunday for eighteen months *The Asian* was a star that shone brightly, both in style and content vying with any top western equivalent. It was however financially always at risk, and when in 1972 President Marcos declared martial law and imprisoned *The Asian's* chief backer, its days were numbered.

At the United Nations

In the third stage of his life Tarzie's career became fully global, based in New York. As the most unlikely and unorthodox international civil servant, he was invited to the UN to be Executive Director of the World Population Year 1974, taking charge of the media programme. He held strong views about the panicky prescriptive western policies on population, which he saw as neo-colonialism. 'The population control world,' he pithily observed, 'is filled with cutters and snippers and stuffers, who always want to stop something.' In eight years with the UN Fund for Population Activities he helped to create a new climate of opinion in which the word control was dropped and the population issue became bound up rather with development, child survival and the rights of women.

In 1980 Jim Grant became Director of Unicef with a brief from President Carter to make the UN less politicised and more an agency for creating change among the poorer nations. Tarzie at once joined Grant as one of a brilliant team of deputies, soon rising to the rank of Assistant Secretary General. With his great communication skills and his passionate wish to help the poor of the world he was a prime exponent of 'social advocacy', which changed Unicef into a fully-fledged welfare and development agency. With a vastly increased budget it soon had the highest profile of any UN body.

'I have used much of my life,' Tarzie once said of himself, 'in bringing good men together.' He was a master at spending UN money on creative conferences and seminars at which he was always an inspirational figure. As the London *Times* wrote, 'He was the antithesis of the greying prudent public servant. He could adopt the sage demeanour of a guru or the passion of an evangelist. He was often irreverent and prepared to be agreeably reckless in his assault on pomp.' He was always a generous spender. A specialist in friendship, Tarzie was known as a lover of women. He had three wives, all in their way exceptional women, and left one daughter and four sons.

He was famous for hanging outside his door at Unicef the powerful, thought-provoking motto, EVERYTHING IS ABOUT SOMETHING ELSE. This was a constant reminder that there was always another perspective, that a deeper look at a situation might bring another solution. It was an extension of his advice to journalists to 'look for the news behind the news'. He rang alarm bells to warn for instance that starvation in Africa was not an event but a process to be watched and foreseen in time for orderly action.

Tarzie can be seen as a central figure in the 'media explosion' of the seventies and eighties, helping to define new ideas and causes that evolved as part of international thinking: social mobilisation, people power, poor power (a Gandhian concept), sustainable development, empowerment of women (though here his macho nature made him somewhat slow). He invented the key concepts 'sufficiency society' and at the end of his life 'participatory communication'.

This last came out of his disillusion with the much-vaunted freedom of the press, and doubt about ability of both the print and broadcast media to bring about real change from materialist values to human ones. He saw Marshall McLuhan's famous dictum, 'The medium is the message,' as a temptation for TV to reduce everything to entertainment. So he turned to what he called the 'non-news media' people who not only spread messages but receive them. They were to be found among the professionals and volunteers in the dramatically increasing number of NGOs; among them were teachers, social workers, priests of various denominations: all those working to bring about a true social democracy outside politics. His daughter Anuradha believes that he intuited what he never lived to see: what he called 'horizontal community communication,' which has now begun to emerge through the Internet. How he would have rejoiced to see the website of OneWorld Online operate as a partnership of all groups working for human rights and sustainable development.

Well-versed as Tarzie became in the truths of the great religions, on spiritual matters he was unfoolable. As one respected Subud member put it, 'He used a bazooka against anything phoney, especially anything to do with God.'

He was a realist too about his own mistakes and faults, giving rise to the comment, 'It was his all-too-human imperfections that made him so attractive. In a way he became a spokesman for us sinners who are still in Subud and doing our best.' His constant travel enabled him to be an ideal servant of the movement, as a brilliant congress chairman, a teller of stories, a healer of disputes. More than once he tried to resign as international chairman but this was never accepted. He was kept there because it was known he had no desire for prestige or authority and would never allow the organisation to be bugged by bureaucracy.

In the summer of 1993 when he was dying of inoperable liver cancer in the home near Oxford of his daughter Anuradha he received both numerous visitors and letters from all over world. Among the latter he rejected anything fulsome, but was pleased by those which showed he had reached a person's feelings, been a mentor or even in some way changed their lives for the better. 'Yes,' he said using a typically earthy phrase, 'I believe I have left some fruitful droppings.'

Hence the title of this little book.

An in-depth biography of Varindra Tarzie Vittachi is at present in preparation.

Life in Inner Space

From *The World Paper*, Boston, September 1991

When I was ten, we had a home in a village in Sri Lanka next to a twelve-acre tropical forest. I've been back there since on a sentimental journey. The forest was no longer there – people have torn it down to build houses.

I had built two tree houses in different parts of the forest. Nothing elaborate – just a plank platform held together with coir-rope (made from the outer husk of coconuts), a bamboo chair and a cot with a rush mat on it. In these roofless houses I spent many hours after school and on weekends being private. In my tree houses I read forbidden books, wrote bad poetry, which we all must have done, fantasised about love and sex and mused about the meanings of life.

Then, when I was thirteen, we moved to the capital, Colombo. It was, to us, a Big City, though it was only a large village, as indeed it still is in many respects today. The first difference I found was that there was no space compared to what I had known in the village, in my forest. So, because there was not outer space, I looked for inner space.

Inside my head and in my inner feelings there was only confusion and a hankering for answers to the 'why' questions gnawing at me night and day. I smothered them as best as I could by reading every book I found in my parents' bookcase, but they never gave me the meanings I sought. The religious teachings at school were no help either. I saw no one at all practising these teachings, though they preached them regularly. It was disenchanting at first and, later, it became the motivation for rebellion against what seemed mass hypocrisy.

That was how it was for me, a youngster in a small town in a small country. No outer space and no meanings within, in inner space. Now multiply that a hundred times, a thousand times, to understand the plight of young people in cities like Tokyo, New York, Mexico City, Bombay, Karachi or Cairo. No outer space at all for them except the scattered basketball pitches and a few seedy parks where you are forbidden to walk or sit on the grass. What does one do if one is fourteen, fifteen or sixteen years old?'

What you do is look inside, as I did, and search for meaning in inner space. But there is nothing there either. It is a secular age, so no religion is taught in schools for fear of offending the separation of state and faith. Not that it would help to find credible meanings any more than my religious education did, but it might at least provoke some thinking about war and peace, life and death and love and hate. That is, provoke thought on human values.

Seeking a means to open their minds, many young people take drugs to look for meaning in inner space. That is why the drug culture's idiom is charged with space words: pad (the launching pad), trip (space trip), spaced out, spaced and so on. Unless parents understand this they will never know why their children become drug users.

Or, if young people are not so bold, they become television addicts. All of us know that addiction lurks within ourselves. Watch a child in front of the box: mouth drooping, eyes glazed, body limp. Spaced out. That glass or plastic screen is the mirror through which Alice fell to find her Wonderland. Indeed, there are wondrous things there: Bugs Bunny, for instance, teaching children how to beat the system, and 100 other heroes reducing the complexities of life to simple black and white situations, good guys and bad guys, we versus they, us versus them, ours versus theirs – ours always coming out on top.

That is certainly one way to find meaning. But are those the meanings we would like to encourage our children to assimilate? Possibly. Otherwise why don't we try to find them human values that are appropriate to our day and age, and absorb them into our own inner lives? It would make a difference to our children. They might even see that we are trying to practise what we preach. That would be a good beginning.

An Educated Person

From his commencement address at
Metropolitan State University, Minnesota, 15 June, 1990

I come from a culture which believes that everything and every man and woman has an inner being and an outer being. Even a word has an inner and an outer – an outer, literal meaning and an inner and deeper meaning. For language is not merely a mechanistic device to express or communicate a wish – like please pass the salt – or state a direction or a fact. That is only the outer function of words. The inner function of words is to speak the truth to ourselves and to others. Words are the language of our dreams about what we love and fear. Words are the repositories of the values we hold most dear. That is why we associate language and education so closely as though they were first-cousins if not brother and sister. That is why when a child in Sri Lanka, my country, needs to be taught to read the first letters, it is done with some ceremony. The child is taken by its parents to the guru down the road and presents him with a handful of betel leaves as a mark of respect and then is taught to read the first letters of the alphabet. That is the beginning of a process of education that continues through life.

I have never doubted that in the beginning was the word. Yes, language is the beginning and middle and end of a conscious life. But this does not mean that those who have learned many languages are necessarily more educated than others. I know that many Americans and Britons who are robustly monolingual feel a sense of inadequacy in Europe and Asia where people almost naturally speak several languages. You may take some comfort from my experience of many United Nations officials of my acquaintance who know six or seven languages and are illiterate in all of them. I once asked Marcel Marceau, that great genius of mime, if there were something he could not mime. He paused for a moment. He had never before been asked that question. Then he replied, 'Yes. You cannot mime a lie.' What I am trying to convey here is my conviction that whatever language you learn and use, it is important to be able to hear its inner resonance, see its many facets and directions, and marvel at its wonderful ambiguities. In that sense every educated person is a poet, even if they have never written a line of verse.

Education is a process, a progression by degree – slow, immeasurably slow most of the time, but occasionally advancing to greater heights, suddenly, by the gift of revelation.

All we can do, therefore, to be educated people is to be willing to see that education is not only an accumulation of information or knowledge, but a process which internalises knowledge and transforms it into being and practice. A university professor may have a very large fund of knowledge but also exist at a very low level of being, while a peasant in an African village may have very little book knowledge but have the being of an angel. Nor is education merely a means of acquiring skill or a formal testimonial of qualification for career advancement. It is that, but much more. Being an educated person is an end in itself. We often measure a man's worth by the hierarchical status he has in the company he works for, by the number of college degrees he has tacked onto his name, or by the size of the material wealth he has acquired. What a travesty of the truth about life to assess a person by what he has rather than by what he is! What nonsense to imagine that education is an acquisition of college degrees or that formal education and wisdom are synonymous!

I have now placed education and wisdom together here and proposed that wisdom is not necessarily identical and synonymous with education, nor is it the product of education, but a quality that grows along with education. The word 'wisdom' has an accretion of many different connotations. I was once on a television program where several of us journalists were interviewing Dr Jonas Salk, the discoverer of the first polio vaccine. He had just published a significant book, *Survival of the Wisest* – as distinct from 'fittest'. An American journalist asked him, 'Dr Salk, what do you mean by wisdom?' I said to myself, 'Aha! This is going to be interesting.' We Asians think we have a monopoly of wisdom. We think that the West is clever, but we are wise. So I said to myself, 'How is this Westerner, Dr Salk, going to respond to this question?' Without batting an eyelid Dr Salk explained: 'I think wisdom is the ability to look at the future retrospectively.'

There you have it. There is an education from the past, knowledge about previous human experience which when internalised into current behaviour and practice gives us pointers to the present and future. In that condition what a person is and what that person does are the same. He is educated and morally right. He is wise.

Let us try now to list the characteristics of an educated person. Because of the clumsiness of the English language, I have to apologise if I use masculine pronouns when I refer to both genders. Forgive me and allow me to use the word man to speak for both men and women. Let me speak for a moment from our Asian wisdom. The word man comes from the Sanskrit *manu*, meaning 'hand of God'. So when I use the English 'man', I am using it in that sense of a human being as an extension of God (not as male vs. female). What then are the special characteristics of an educated person – an educated 'man'?

* He will never make a display of his knowledge.
* He is the sort of person who can amuse himself when he is alone in a room or alone in a crowded plane on a long Pacific flight.
* He will have developed a habit of scepticism. (In my reading of the New Testament, Doubting Thomas has always seemed the most educated one among Christ's disciples.)
* He will ask the question 'why?' more often than he asks other questions such as 'how?' and 'how much?'
* He will ask himself, Is it right to do this or that? rather than, Can this or that be done?
* He will be excited by symbols and miserable until he explodes the meanings out of them, because symbols are the keys to culture.
* He will constantly look for perspective and context in his search for understanding, because there is no meaning without a relationship.
* He will not be satisfied with how things look but will want to know how things are.
* He will bear in mind that most people's view of the world is determined by what they want to protect, be it power, job security or status.
* He will know that in politics and diplomacy everything is about something else.
* He will not commit the pathetic fallacy of believing that the absence of proof is proof of absence.
* He will look at the world from a moral viewpoint but avoid being moralistic and self-righteous. (I feel that I can cope with a sinner but not with a person who is self-righteous.)
* He will be willing to defend other men's right to choose as rigorously as he defends his own. The mark of a

human being is having the faculty of choice.
* He will be able to empathise with the tribulations of other people even though they are strangers in looks and culture. There is only one human race.
* He will understand that human relationships are about caring and sharing and equity.

And, most important of all, the educated man will know and feel that he is not living in a self-sufficient, self-motivated nation-state as our nineteenth-century ancestors did, but in a single, intricately intermeshed world, in a mosaic of peoples which makes a wonderfully varied but related culture of one human race.

Reporting the Good News

From the Arjuna Column in *The Asian*, April 1972

All journalists learn very early that bad news makes news. Human relationships – and that is what newspapers are about – usually produce bad news because misunderstanding, prejudice and hate relate people much more to one another than love. All 'love' stories, if you take a sharp look at their content and theme, are actually stories of the failure to communicate, of prejudice, hatred, jealousy, the primal wish to hurt and humiliate others – particularly those we claim we love. This love we talk so much about is, more often than not, aggression motivated by self-love. That is why most lovers demand all the time: 'Do you love me? Do you love me?' What does it mean? It means: 'Do you love me as much as I love me?'

We on *The Asian* are trying to tell the other side of the human story too, to report the 'good news'. Rice is as newsy as riots, we feel. A good job done by a government is as good a news story as some particularly vicious abuse of power. A thaw between enemies is as important to report as the events that froze them into hostility. Efforts to overcome the burden of poverty people have carried for centuries is as much news as the material triumphs of the rich.

I remember being told by a cynical Fleet Street editor that there were only five things that made news: sex, money, health, crime and other people's troubles. Like all such apothegms, it is only ninety percent true. He left out one important field of news – the wish of the human spirit to get out from under its material burden. Is that not what we give that big name to? Culture?

Lost in the Fog

To a Subud audience, 1990

Pak Subuh once spoke to me about the difference between Destiny and Fate. He said, 'Most people think that Destiny and Fate are the same thing. They are not.' He said, 'This is the line of destiny, this is the line of fate. Destiny is God's will for each one of us; everything we need, the line of destiny brings to us. But fate is the line on which we live, subject to all the lower forces. So the line of destiny represents what should happen to us and could happen to us, and the line of fate represents what does happen to us. On the line of fate we are demanding this, we are wanting this and that, and we quarrel with one another. Thus we put a fog in front of us with our passions. And so the postman who is bringing these packages that you need cannot find his way to you. These packages contain everything you need. You need a good house to live in – that is a package. You need a good husband or wife – that is a package. But because of the way we are with all our ambitions and our quarrelling, these packages have got lost.'

'So what do you do about it?' Bapak said. 'You must thin down, you must reduce this fog by doing the *latihan* and by *prihatin* (self-abnegation). Then the postman can find his way to you.'

An Oblique Way of Explaining Subud

From his Arjuna column in *The Asian*, 1972

The teacher was saying that human beings had been so profoundly overpowered by material forces that they had lost contact with the Great Life Force, which envelops and penetrates everything in the universe. One of his audience asked whether this contact was still available and where he should look for it. It has always been available, said the teacher, and if you are willing to receive it, you will. Will I find it in a system of spiritual knowledge? the man asked. No, replied the teacher, the worship of God through contact with the Great Life Force is not a system but a technique. The questioner asked what the difference was between 'system' and technique.

The teacher explained it thus: You want to build a house. So you draw a blueprint. This is a true and accurate statement of intention about the way the house should be built. But it is not a house. And you cannot build the house from a blueprint because you are not an engineer. Only an engineer can understand the blueprint and follow it. Why is it that the engineer can build it and you cannot? Because the engineer has technique. The blueprint is the system. The contact with the Great Life Force is the technique.

Play the Game of Paradigms

From the Arjuna column in *The Asian*, 1971

I am	You are	He is
a patriot	a guerrilla	a terrorist
virile	passionate	a sex maniac
firm	stubborn	bloody minded
a philosopher	a visionary	a crack-pot
a shrewd businessman	a smooth operator	a swindler
a gourmet	someone who likes their food	a glutton
I was a star	you have seen better days	he is a has-been
a journalist	a reporter	a muckraker
I have a drink problem	you are a drunk	he is an alcoholic
I have no secrets	you are indiscreet	he is a blabbermouth

Why War?

Subud World Congress, Sydney, 1988

As a very young journalist two colleagues and I interviewed Jean Paul Sartre. In the course of the conversation I asked him for his definition of existentialism. His answer was a surprising question, 'Do you like war?' I said, 'Of course not.' The other two journalists said the same. Sartre went on, 'Neither do I like war. But there is war. Let us go out and ask the first one hundred people you meet, "Do you like war?" Everyone will say of course not. But there is war. That is what existentialism means to me.'

When I next met Bapak I asked him, 'Bapak, why is there war?' Bapak said, 'Because there is war in yourself.' And this is what we have been discovering in these Congress sessions. If we are honest enough to admit that, we begin with ourselves. That is why we are here in Subud – because we have already declared to ourselves that we are aware of the need to change and are willing to make an effort to change.

A Bill of Responsibilities

October 1975

In 1976, two hundred years of American independence was to be celebrated on the Fourth of July. The previous autumn Tarzie, calling himself an 'invited cuckoo in the Bicentennial nest', joined a number of prominent like-minded citizens to promote a Bill of Responsibilities as one of the main features of the celebrations. Here are some extracts from a draft paper he prepared.

Responsibilities are what we owe to ourselves. Rights are what other people believe we owe to them. Responsibilities are owed by all of us for the sole reason that we are human.

These debts exist even if we have never considered their existence and even if, having recognised them, we choose not to acknowledge them.

Only human beings have the faculty of conscious choice. When we choose to recognise our responsibilities we vindicate our assumption that we human beings have a right to use the resources of this planet to suit our purposes.

If we choose to assert our right to use the planet without considering our responsibilities we bring about chaos in this world – the degradation of our species and the spoliation of our resources.

All human societies – local communities, ethnic groups, religious denominations, nations, regional associations and international bodies – are good only insofar as the individuals they comprise are able to recognise their individual responsibilities. When many, if not most, members of such an association are able to do so, it is able to respect its particular purposes and to respect also the particular purposes of other human associations.

Being responsible means, simply, being respectful. This sense of respect begins with ourselves. If we respect ourselves we value our individuality and understand the value of the individuality of others. Self-respect leads to considerateness and to a recognition of responsibilities.

The recognition of our responsibilities, to be more than ideologically valuable, must be effectual, and so needs to be substantiated in individual and communal action. Recognition presupposes that we have the means of discriminating between what is considerate and what is inhumane, between what is altruistic and what is purely self-serving, what is respectful and what is contemptuous.

Never before have we had as many tools and skills as we now own which can be used to produce and distribute the food needed to prevent any child, woman or man from being hungry; but never before have there been more hungry people in this world.

We have the means to provide clothing, housing, education and health for all the people now alive, and more, but we deal with these needs as 'crises' because we have been thoughtlessly willing to tolerate the distortions of abundance and misery we see about us everywhere. We avoid making the necessary choices and decisions by dividing ourselves into 'optimists' and 'pessimists', ingenuously expecting solutions to emerge in those semantic refuges.

We talk more about international peace than we ever did before in history but the international arms trade has never been bigger.

We have the technical means to sharpen our faculty of

foresight and to recall the experience of the past; but never before have we been so blind to the past and the future.

We have never before had the capacity we now have of recording accurately, recalling swiftly, and disseminating widely the information we need to understand the complex relationships and trends of our lives; but these means are used too often to wound rather than heal, to entrench conflict rather than uproot its causes, to widen the gap in understanding, and to serve superficial and self-serving ends.

The widespread nature, frequency and magnitude of the crises that all nations are embattled with are clear symptoms of the need for realising that the values and attitudes that rule our society and its relationship with other people, our environment, and the material resources of our planet, are irrational and inept. The problems of poverty, hunger, environmental pollution, population growth, political accommodation, ethnic differences, energy, raw material supplies and the use of the sea-bed are global problems impinging on our prospects of responsible evolution and even of our very survival.

A courageous change of stance is called for – from one that is preoccupied with our rights as individuals and as a nation to one that recognises our responsibilities in a world in which the ferment for change is as pressing as it was in the time when our nation was born. But, after 200 years of experience as a nation, we find ourselves in a more complex and interdependent world in which particular interests must be correlated with the common interests of humanity everywhere.

At our birth as a nation we were preoccupied with Rights, because only by their assertion could we survive. Now, in our maturity, we must assert our Responsibilities and give substance to them because that is the only way that our civilisation can survive.

In the event, nothing came of this initiative to celebrate the Bicentennial in a meaningful way. It was a time of Presidents Nixon and Ford and the nation was just recovering from the final humiliation in Vietnam, the fall of Saigon. The emphasis was all on heritage and nostalgia. What people mostly remember from that year was the great congregation of tall ships that came from all over the world to New York Harbour.

Sayings

Life is never about either/or but about and/and.

The poor are the experts on poverty.

People's perceptions of the world are usually determined by what they seek to protect. And language is frequently a means not of revealing but of masking our thoughts and distorting the inconvenient opinions of others.

Never grovel because people are famous or powerful. Read tyrants as though you were a detective, and learn to say no.

It's not global warming that will destroy us, it's gullibility.

I was all the right things – a majority man, a Singhalese, a Buddhist, the right caste, oh everything. But defending the minority rights was not on. *(After being forced into exile in 1961.)*

One gets great lessons from history in that, however long it takes, the power of the powerless can change history's course. When the powerless get together in a chorus of protest, armed with nothing more than their strong will for survival and for the growth of their children, the centre of gravity can be moved.

Responsibilities are what we owe to ourselves. Rights are what other people believe we owe them. Responsibilities are owed by all of us for the sole reason that we are human.

It is important to learn to work with all kinds of people, including bureaucrats. You must learn to carry water on both your shoulders. (*Answer to a negative remark about bureaucrats.*)

* * *

Always take a sideways look at things, then you will see them better.

Information is not what is said but what is understood. I view the world with a mixture of sardonic humour and unquenchable optimism. (As editor of *The Asian*.)

Journalism remains my love – but it's a jade, because the paper is always owned by someone else.

When I need to assess the work of a human being, as I must as a journalist, I find myself using the touchstone: is the man capable of gratitude? Does his work have the feel of gratitude?

Development journalism is not pro- or anti-government, but pro-people.

Communication without transformation is gossip.

Facts do not necessarily tell the true story.

The death of a journalist diminishes our profession. The death of a good journalist, one of the brightest and the best, diminishes civilisation. (*On the silencing by murder in Colombo of Richard de Zoysa in 1990.*)

Subud is not a teaching, but it is a great learning.

Go ahead and be responsible in the world, but feel in yourself first what you are able to do.

Laugh more: it brings more oxygen to the brain and lightens the load there.

We Subud members should try to be courteous to everyone, all the time, for that is a sign of true, inner human culture.

All of us who have been assigned to perform a task have responsibilities, but none of us has authority. The Subud organisation is not a power structure but a service. That is the greatest challenge Bapak placed before us: how to carry our responsibility without authority.

Favourite quotations from others

Reduce your wants and supply your needs. (*Gandhi*)

There is only one thing worse than cruelty and that is cowardice. (*Gandhi*)

Never doubt that a small group of thoughtful, committed people can change the world. Indeed it is the only thing that ever has. (*Margaret Mead*)

Freedom is nothing but responsibility – unless there is responsibility there is no freedom. (*Simone Weil*)

Have you not noticed that we judge ourselves by our intentions, others by their deeds? (*J. G. Bennett*)

We have not inherited the earth from our ancestors. We have borrowed it from our children. (*An old African saying.*)

Kissinger on Interdependence

At the 6th World Conference of Physicians for the Prevention of Nuclear War, Cologne, May 1986.

They keep telling us in this super-power world that the world is interdependent. I first heard this word used in public in 1973, in December, when the so-called Arab oil-embargo had been launched. This is what the Americans called an oil crisis, and the Arabs called it an oil opportunity. I remember reading that Henry Kissinger, then the mighty Henry Kissinger, had said to the Nato foreign ministers meeting in Washington DC that the world is interdependent. And I asked myself how is it possible? Henry Kissinger speaking of the brotherhood and the sisterhood of man? How is it possible? I don't believe this. And I followed this man right round the world wherever he spoke; at the Food Conference in Rome, at the Nairobi Amcad Conference, I heard him say it: 'The world is interdependent.'

And then I began to understand what he was meaning by this. He was actually saying, 'Look, you Arabs, you have oil, we have a need for it. If you do not give it to us at prices we consider reasonable, watch it!' That was what interdependence was. And he taught me a lesson, and I am grateful for that, that interdependence without equity is rubbish. It only means deepening dependency of the poorer and the weaker.

Tarzie Takes on Marshall McLuhan

1986

The epigram 'The Medium is the Message' is insidious and troubling. It was intended as a complementary description of the nature of video communication. This was so 'hot' and mesmeric that it overwhelmed the viewer with its power. It was encyclopean, reducing the pluralistic reality of the world to a single viewpoint.

McLuhan's slick line was swiftly adopted by the media whose purposes it served so well … Television networks had been assailed for two decades for their superficial handling of news, their way of vulgarising and distorting reality.

They had closed ranks against formidable critics such as Roberto Rossellini, the great neo-realistic film director who in the last years of his life refused to use television for entertainment. He spent years making some superbly insightful TV films like *Cosimo de Medici* about the origins of capitalism. But his films were never shown in the US, because they defied the almighty 'ratings' principle on which the TV networks subsist. *Cosimo* would not sell cornflakes and deodorants.

But then, with McLuhan's ex-cathedra statement the networks no longer needed to feel embarrassed by the tawdriness of their message. They *were* the message. They were not only a channel of communication but also its contents.

Does the fact that the networks in the US, Britain, Italy and Japan devote five minutes of their daily newscasts to world affairs make this world of ours a global village? Does the fact that *Dallas* and *Dynasty* – as well as similar masterpieces of TV producers specialising in tipping over flat stones and finding golden toads copulating underneath – go over big in Colombo, Cairo, Dacca and Dakar, enable these Third World audiences to understand the culture of the affluent US? Or does it just reinforce counter-stereotypes of rich, brawling, lusty, corrupt and of course, 'typical' Americans interested in the 'bottom line', in every sense of the word … ?

What is to be done? Alas, nothing I can think of except exercise the only choice left: switch the damn thing off.

The situation, perhaps, has not turned out as badly as Varindra had expected. Ed.

The Environment and the Invironment

To a Subud audience, 1992

The United Nations Conference on Environment and Development to be held in June, 1992, in Rio de Janeiro, will be the biggest meeting ever held in history – certainly in terms of numbers. Some forty to sixty thousand are expected to attend. It is a gathering of the tribes. When do the tribes gather? When they all perceive that disaster threatens all of them, especially their children who must continue the race.

But it is very important, I think, not to expect Rio to solve the problems of the environment. It may set some guidelines and produce some laws to protect the environment but the work really begins after the tribes scatter and go home. The work is at home where people live. There is nothing more global and nothing more local than the environment. Most of the work needs to be done at home, in our homes, in our neighbourhoods, in our heads, and most importantly in our inner. Most people, when they talk of the environment, think only of the natural environment of the land and the sea and the air, and the pollution and depletion of its life-supporting resources. That concern is unquestionably valid and important to all people in all countries, rich or poor.

But there is a second environment: the environment of poverty in which three billion human beings live, one billion of whom are actually destitute. Poverty, wretchedness and the worst, hopelessness, is their daily environment. It is useless telling a Nepali hill family not to cut the forest for firewood because it creates land erosion and depletes the atmosphere, unless we are prepared to see that they have some alternative form of affordable energy. It is useless to preach environmental protection to people who are so desperate that they feel that their lives are worthless and that their children's future is hopeless. Unless the so-called global community is prepared to share a fair proportion of its surplus wealth and its technology with the developing world, all the verbiage now being expended on ecological sentiment will amount to very little.

And such an enormous change will not happen by some technological miracle, some *deus ex machina*, which will be sent in the nick of time by the gods of science to resolve the tragic drama in a denouement with a happy ending. It can only happen if we acknowledge that there is a vital *third* environment which I like to call the *invironment* (I am indebted to Reynold Feldman for this term) – the inner values which we need for survival and development of all living beings who inhabit this planet.

We have misread our holy books and have acted as though we humans had a God-given mandate to abuse the planet when He reportedly gave us 'Dominion over the fish of the sea, and over the fowl of the air, and over the cattle, and over all the earth, and over every creeping thing that creepeth upon the earth'. We were given hands and brains to *use* the earth's treasure, not to plunder them as vandals do. We alone have done it. We alone can undo it. No other creature fouls its own nest. We do. Perhaps we still have time to clean it up.

We can sense the truth with our *latihan* and let it touch our thoughts and our words and our actions in our families, in our workplaces and in our communities so that we develop a respectful relationship with ourselves and our environment.

We can spread the word that unless we change our relationships with one another, with our neighbours, and with our ambiences, life on Earth will soon become unsustainable. In the old language of the Bible we need to 'repent'. And repentance is not just a matter of beating our breasts and promising to be better in the future. It means to have a new mind – what the Greek bible called 'metanoia' – a new mind with new values. And these new values, we shall find, are some of the oldest values in the world.

We can confine our energies to our own selves and to our families. But it won't do. We can join up with other groups outside Subud who are working well to bring about these transformations. We need to move mountains and we can't do it by ourselves.

And we can write. That is the way I contribute.

War, pollution, cruelty, injustice, greed, fear, jealousy – all these are the pollutants of the invironment. That is where we need to begin to clean up. Those are the forces we need to surrender.

Isn't that where we begin?

The Inner Change of Subud

Bima, Issue 5, 1972

Where will the inner change come from to hasten, guide, manage human societies in the new epoch? That is what people, the young and the old, are looking for. Some will look for it in books; some try to persuade or cajole the turbulent mind to find peace through meditation; some cling to the beards and words of the new gurus; some make efforts to revive old faiths. But we try to find a way through the inner guidance of the *latihan*. It is a humble way ...

Cracking Myths at the UN

1990

Why are so many donor governments becoming increasingly reluctant to continue playing the development game? The annual increases in their contributions is still rising, but at a slower rate, just about keeping pace with inflation. They sound as if they will continue paying lip service to the mythology to which the Lester Pearson Commission gave the name of 'Partners in Development'. It was never a partnership in the sense of an equal or even an equitable relationship. How can there be equality of attitude between the man with his hand on the purse and the man with his hand held out for a piece of it? Of course there is a lot of language used in these aid transactions and plenty of old-fashioned minuets are danced when the deal is signed. But underneath all that balderdash is the reality of lofty giver and lowly recipient.

Many times I have sat on the podium representing Unicef at those pledging conferences where donors come to promise what they intend to contribute to various agencies for the coming year. These events emit the reek of an old-time slave market. Five million for UNDP, four million for Unicef, three and a bit for UNFPA and so on from the rich countries and the agency representatives sit up there dry-washing their hands with grovelling gratitude all the while calculating how much less than their expectations the pledges are. Meanwhile, shamed over the years of receiving 'development assistance', the developing countries, shamefacedly express their thanks for the munificence of the West and, just to show that they are not outright beggars, squeak their pitiful pledges of 230 dollars and 79 cents or whatever will get them on the donor's list. What I found most revolting was the hypocrisy of the whole exercise. What is the point of pretending that there is a sort of equal and dignified partnership deal that is being worked out?

There is a lot of diplomatic cant at such United Nations meetings, especially from the receiver nations, about the great impetus to national improvement provided by foreign aid. At most one or two UN agencies, through whom these monies go for country programmes, have helped receiver governments to spend that money well so that some beneficial result can be shown in a reasonable time. The rest spend most of it on themselves.

To give added piquancy to the aid relationship is the verifiable fact that the donor countries have a very solid commercial reason to prolong the development aid game though they know that it has yielded very little development. They have found that foreign aid is good business. Most of the goods and services which the agencies buy for their development programmes are imported from the donor nations. Britain, for instance, makes a handsome commercial profit from its contribution to Unicef. So does Japan, France and, more recently, the United States. Most of the millions contributed for spreading the use of oral rehydration therapy and contraceptives in Egypt returns to the United States in the form of payments to 'communication' experts, back-up staff and equipment sold. The Egyptians get a few humble jobs and some experience which is largely irrelevant and, therefore, unsustainable without continuing dependency.

If the Secretary General is serious about his intention to improve the performance of the UN development agencies this is where he should be concentrating.

Instead, he has so far been working on 'restructuring' the bureaucracy: one of the UN's most popular pastimes over the past four decades. It seems he is gung-ho about 'merging' the administrations of the UNDP, UNFPA and Unicef. If inefficiency at the core is what he is concerned about he must surely see that merging the inefficient with the efficient will only serve to reduce the level of performance to the lowest common denominator. The deeper problems are not structural but political. The rules of the development game and its values need to be changed before there is any real development. Change is needed on the donors' side as well as on the recipients' side.

Is it Enough?

Pate Institute Bulletin, June 1989

Concern about the future of our planet has now become an everyday news story. The far-reaching impact of rapid population growth, global warming, ozone depletion and decimated forest land has become the stuff of cover features and prime time television. It is all to the good that the long, urgent pleas of environmentalists are now reaching a mass audience.

But is it enough? And will it last? One merely has to remember the celebration of 'Earth Day' nearly two decades ago. It was conceived in a great fanfare, and when it was over, we simply went back to business. It was like honouring our mother once a year with breakfast in bed, as penance for abusing her mercilessly during the remaining 364 days. Today, Mother Earth needs our support as never before.

The Philosophy of Unicef

Extracts from a speech in 1986, often referred to,
on 'Forty Years of Progress in Unicef'

The character of childhood and growth has been drastically altered since Unicef was born, by the pervasive influence of television, by the dissolution of the extended family, and by the tendency of textbook expertise to replace a moral framework for child rearing. Add to this the tendency for the care of the health and welfare of children to become more and more institutionalised, so that many of the traditional roles of parenting have been relegated to remote and impersonal systems, and it is not difficult to account for the dereliction of the ancient human ethos of regarding the degree of care for children as the most sensitive measure of civilised behaviour.

Behind all Unicef-assisted programmes are strategies of action – whether they involve the drilling of wells for clean water; providing access to vaccination; supporting primary education; promoting breast-feeding, improved weaning practices, and child growth; controlling diarrhoea diseases; advising on nutrition, hygiene and environmental sanitation; training traditional birth attendants; improving women's literacy and ability to generate their own income; advocating birth spacing for the benefit of both mother and child; or devising audio-visual materials to disseminate information – is the aim of motivating and empowering families to be better able to look after their children.

Unicef's constant interaction with governments, and with non-governmental organisations and individuals and the media, is intended to generate and sustain a constant ambience of conscious attention to children's needs, a pervasive and permanent climate of caring. In the absence of such a public ethic of concern, children are likely to be last, not first, on the world's development agenda.

Children's needs fall across a wide spectrum of priorities which include survival and life-sustaining needs such as nutritive food and clean water; life-protecting needs such as safety against physical and mental abuse and damage and preventive care against disease; life-enriching needs such as knowledge of social values; life embellishing need such as play and fantasy and life 'development' needs such as education and vocational training.

Unicef recognises the importance of all these varying elements of child care but also recognises that Unicef alone cannot deal effectively with all these needs. Unicef is only a handful of people with a handful of money, approximately a million dollars a day for programmes in over a hundred developing countries. But fortunately, Unicef, as the world's children's agency, is blessed with many potential allies who are committed to the care and protection of children and some of them are experts in various aspects of this field of development who are ready and willing and able to work in many areas of children's concerns – as in fact they have done with considerable verve and distinction for many years. Indeed some private institutions are better suited than an intergovernmental agency to deal with certain needs such as protection from the consequences of armed conflict. Unicef's clearest roles are those of catalyst, disseminator of productive ideas rooted in experience, and general advocate for the children of the world.

The People Factor

As Unicef reaches its fortieth anniversary there are propitious signs suggesting that people everywhere are increasingly willing to support positive action on a broad front for the benefit of children seen to be in trouble, particularly from an obviously major set-back or 'loud' emergency. The surge of popular fervour for Africa, which followed as a response to the media coverage of the famine in Ethiopia in October 1984, moved governments to contribute impressively large amounts of money and supplies for the emergency relief programmes managed by the United Nations. Private voluntary organisations, too, received massive support for their African efforts from corporations and individuals. The most successful fund-raising events in history – Band Aid and Live Aid – provided the opportunity for pop musicians and their fans to mobilise not only money but an unprecedented level of solidarity with Africa. The song, 'We are the world, we are the children,' which raised funds in so many countries, was a musical expression of the profound human capacity for empathy.

World citizens clearly insist today on a meaningful response to major loud emergencies. The scale of these public responses made it clear beyond doubt that though the official world and the mass media may suffer from what is now called 'aid fatigue', people do not. When people are informed about other people's urgent needs and learn that something can be done about them, they dig deep down into their natural well of humane feelings and reach new levels of generosity and understanding.

Social Mobilisation – the powerless as a force for good

Hopefully, history will record the mid-1980s as the years

in which the power of the powerless as a force for good was recognised across the globe – not only for desirable political change, but also for bringing about social change. Social mobilisation as a powerful strategy of development came increasingly into its own in 1986. Widespread recognition of the nature of the African crisis, not only as a 'loud' emergency calling for rescue efforts but also as a long-term 'silent' emergency calling for a development response, came about in 1986. The vital need to adjust international and national financial and economic policies to take into account the human needs of valuable groups began to be acknowledged in 1986, and some manufacturing countries have begun to take action accordingly. Even the language of policy debates in the international community softened in 1986, indicating that hard heads, too, can be moved by humane considerations. If Unicef has learned anything from its fortieth year – and from all its forty years – it is that even in the darkest times, hope for a better world for children remains undimmed.

Tarzie Passes on a Parable

To the Boston Subud group, summer 1992

Bapak [Pak Subuh] once told me a story which I have no shame in repeating often, because it's a parable and people can learn a lot from parables. He told it this way, addressing me: 'Varindra, you keep running; you run and run every day with all these wild animals, tigers and lions and creepy crawly snakes and spiders all chasing you. Then you come to a precipice, with a deep abyss, but it is only ten feet across to the other side. Even a boy of ten can jump this. There is open green land on the other side and no wild animals, no creepy crawlies anywhere in sight. A wonderful place and maybe a white cottage far away. But you cannot surrender your fear of jumping this abyss. You want to but you dare not.

But God is merciful. He drops a rope from above, just over the lip of the abyss. All you have to do is to hold the rope and swing yourself across. But this rope is six inches above your ordinary reach. All you have to do is to jump these six inches. But you dare not. You dare not surrender your fear. So you turn around and keep running and running, and all these creatures are still chasing after you.

I try to remember this story before every *latihan* [the surrender exercise] so that my willingness to surrender, my surrender will be six inches deeper.

When Bapak originally told me this parable he went on to ask: What do you surrender? Have you got big estates? Have you got a lot of power? Have you got a lot of money? Or a lot of sins? Are you capable of big sins? Have you waged war? Have you murdered anyone? You are incapable [of that].

Then what is it you have to surrender? Those things in

yourself which you despise in others: envy, jealousy, the habit of gossip, the habit of distrust, habitual irritability, the wish to be holier than anyone else, the habit of wanting to humiliate and so on.

What you have to surrender is what you have contempt for. Fear, meaningless fear. Will my child return from school today? If I lose my job what will I do? You know, this kind of rubbish goes on in our heads all the time. That is what we have to surrender.

Brave Start to Reporting the Truth on Sustainable Development

From a talk at the Pate Institute for Human Survival,
Conneticut, October 1989

I have just completed a newspaperman's journey round
the world to observe the quantity and quality of the
media's reporting of sustainable development. The
United Nations Development Programme commissioned
me to take a particular look at the level of public
awareness in Asia, the home of half the world's people,
of the need to find ways of using the natural resources of
the planet without befouling and degrading it for our
children and grandchildren.

Suddenly, it seems, the world's Press, both the print
and broadcast Press, after three decades of neglect and
even contempt towards the work of a few individuals
like Barry Commoner, René Dubois, Barbara Ward, Lester
Brown, Wangari Mattai of Kenya, James Lovelock and a
few scattered groups like the International Union for the
Conservation of Nature, the Chipko Movement in India,
the Greens in Europe and the Hopi Indians in America,
have woken up to the realisation that the dreadful state
of our small planet, the crimes we have been committing
against it and our own chances of survival, make good
human stories, good 'copy'.

In every Asian country they have established a
National Forum of Environmental Journalists. Almost
every day there are stories and features in the *Mainichi
Shimbun*, the *South China Morning Post* in Hongkong, the
Philippine Bulletin, the *Indonesian Observer*, the *Thai Rath*,
The Ceylon Daily News, the *Dacca Observer*, the *Pakistan
Dawn* and *Pakistan Times*, the *Indian Express*, the *Katmandu*

Motherland and the *Himalaya Magazine* about the ravages of industrial pollution, the hectic denudation of the rainforests and the pollution of the rivers and fishing grounds. In Bangladesh, the National Forum of Environmental Journalists have succeeded in preventing their government from importing the garbage of the United States – for the profit of some clever industrialist – and have stopped the prawn and shrimp industry from destroying the mangrove swamps in which the rudimentary life-supporting fauna of the people around the river is spawned.

Is it time for *Time* magazine to take a bow for the applause they received for producing that excellent issue last winter in which they celebrated, not the customary Man of the Year, but the Planet of the Year and courageously broke new journalistic ground by daring to flout the Time-honoured principle that advocacy of good causes is not the business of the media. Should we compliment the BBC and PBS for consistently putting on such documentaries as *The Fragile Mountain* and the annual *Global Report* , which have dealt superbly with the terrible destructiveness that we have wrought on our environment? Yes, of course it is time to cheer.

But I offer only one hearty cheer, not the traditional three. Am I being ungenerous? No, I don't think so, but I leave it to your judgement. I am only exercising my prerogative as a veteran journalist of being sceptical and also my natural inclination towards the truth that underlies the facts. All I can concede now is that we have made a belated beginning. But this beginning, is no more than a brave start. The truth is that most of the reporting is superficial in that it does not even attempt to confront the deeper, more fundamental issues of environmental degradation.

This superficiality, I submit, is the result of our

familiar tendency to follow power as the source of news. On environmental matters the sources of power are the politicians in their high offices, the business moguls in their executive suites, and the scientists in their chromium laboratories. They hold all the secrets of the environment. The line of reasoning is that since it is science and its technological products that, while yielding the fruits of what we call 'Progress', also caused the deleterious side-effects such as the pollution of the seas and the land and the air, as well as the spendthrift exploitation of the Earth's natural resources, we must look to science and technology to produce the remedies.

That approach may even be true as far as it goes. But, I plead, it does not go far enough. It is a grossly one-dimensional approach to a multi-layered and complex question. It deals with only one aspect, albeit an important aspect of the problem – the Outer Environment: the pollution of the eco-system and the exhaustion of its natural resources.

Even at the level of the Outer, there is another desperately important dimension which is not being adequately reported or understood by the media: the dimension of gross poverty and gross underdevelopment in which three-quarters of the human race subsists. One third of them, nearly a billion, live in the environment of obscene destitution, side by side with equally obscene abundance. The homes of the Beautiful People of Manila, in Das Marengas Village and Forbes Park, are not far from the Smoky Mountain of Tondo where thousands of Filipino families root out an existence from that burning hill of garbage, the effluence of the affluent. The sign of the Big Mac restaurant in Bangkok, frequented by the children with money in their designer jeans, rises proudly out of a purulent slum.

What sustainable development for them, and their

parents? What is the 'environment' for the millions who must hang on to life by their teeth and finger nails? But that is in the Outer Dimension of concern. We journalists do write about that sort of life occasionally with a sort of furtive look of curiosity. That is about all. Poverty is not an event but a process, and we don't know how to report process. And the UN agencies piously relegate the people of that dimension to the ill-funded charity of the NGOs. Sociologists have a field day grubbing about those dark and dirty habitats of half-humans, but the eyes of the media glaze over when they read their reports.

Deeper still, the dimension of the Inner Environment which, ignored by everyone except some irredeemable and unrepentant crazies like myself, is the source of the prime cause of, and the possible remedy for, our ecological problems. I refer, of course, to the ethical dimension, the values which determine the quality of our lives. For hundreds of years we have become increasingly secularised in our search for scientific 'proof' and for the necessary freedom from the bigotry and irrational dogma that had accumulated around the wisdom of our great teachers. We wanted to free ourselves from the priestcraft and magic which had engendered those false and often cruel doctrines. But, sadly, we have thrown the baby away with the bath water. We have discarded the values which qualified us to call ourselves 'human' and chased breathlessly after the new gods of progress and their 'pragmatic' (which means amoral) promises of the 'good life' of production consumerism and ever-increasing profit. We have stopped asking, is it right or is it wrong? And is it good or is it bad? We ask instead: does it work or not? Is it profitable or not? Is it cost-efficient or not?

And so we raped our forests for the building industry and blamed it on the poor peasants who have no other energy to cook their food and heat their houses. So we extracted the coal from the belly of the Earth and left the land around inert like the moonscape. So we dumped the effluence of our cities into the waters forgetting that the Koran and the Hadiths of Muhammad had actually enjoined us 'not to throw our waste into still waters nor even into running water'. And we produced only to consume more and more, forgetting that the Buddha had told us that human degradation comes from greed and envy. We went out and multiplied as the Bible told us to but we ignored the second part of that advice: 'Replenish the earth'.

Unless all of us who are vocally concerned with a sustainable future for humanity – politicians, scientists, journalists and people in their communities – recognise that we need to return to a value-based life, we will not be able to return this Earth to our children in a state in which their lives on it will be worth living.

Participatory Communication for Sustainable Development

Written with Hamza Dom de Silva, 1993

Efforts made by the international community to assist developing countries to improve their economies and thereby able to raise the living conditions of their people have, by and large, failed. Economic development has been achieved, particularly in a few countries in Asia known as the Little Tigers. They are, in varying degrees, centrally controlled nations of the Left or the Right where no dissidence (in my view the first Human Right) was permitted. Development, as designed by the government, was rammed through without any consultation with the people. (The human cost of this kind of success, in my view, is not worth paying.)

In more open developing countries central planning of the social-democratic kind has been tried for forty years. They have failed to deal with the basic cause of maldevelopment – poverty – and have had only spotty successes in dealing with malnutrition, low levels of education, especially among women, unbridled population growth, rampant environmental degradation and spoliation of natural resources, the widening gap between rich and poor, cultural pollution, preventable illness – and many of them are now confronting the new scourge of Aids.

The principal reason for this failure is that the elites who take all the political and economic decisions and draw up development plans have taken the 'supply' approach to development and social change, which they believe they can control at the centre, rather then the 'demand' approach, which is based on the people at the periphery, rural or urban. These are still regarded as rather dim-witted, inarticulate, passive creatures waiting for the bones of development to drop into their supplicating hands. This is much as the imperial governments used to regard them. This time the angel who is expected to bring this manna down from heaven is not the colonial power but foreign aid.

Without the informed participation of people as principal actors in the drama of the development of their own life and growth, no real development can take place. Political democracy is not genuine until it goes hand in hand with economic democracy.

Economic democracy and active popular participation cannot be achieved without democratic communication. This approach is based on a continuing dialogue with people, using easy and fairly cheap modern technology such as video and audio tape, interactive meetings, face-to-face conversation with graphic aids, and the training of grass-root and sidewalk communicators to use these techniques to express themselves to the change agent as well as their own communities. They thus become change agents themselves in their own neighbourhoods. The whole becomes an exchange of knowledge and information rather than a one-way transaction. The chief means of managing participatory communication programmes should be NGOs, not state officials.

Another Kind of Love

From the Arjuna column in *The Asian* January, 1973

There are two kinds of love. One kind of love makes you feel 'I love this' or 'I love him' in which there are always two things, the lover and the person loved. This kind of love comes from the heart, which is also the source of hate. All that is certain in this world is that everything changes. So as lovers change each one asks, 'Is this the same one as I loved before? He or she is so different now.' And this is where the pain begins.

There is another kind of love in which there is no sense of possession or even passion, and one only feels, 'This is love.' There is only recognition of value. There are not two things involved, no lover and loved, only love which transpires. When time passes and change takes place there is no pain.

A Conscious Culture of Caring

From the draft of a lecture to the Harvard Divinity School, 1993

In the autumn of 1993 Tarzie was asked to deliver the prestigious de Witts Lecture at the Harvard Divinity School. He was the first non-theologian to be invited to do so, but he was too ill and instead sent a message to the Harvard meeting which was read posthumously.

People of every spiritual persuasion have long thought that the old orthodoxies will no longer do. Claiming special omnipotence or virtuousness for one of the religions that have existed for the last three thousand years will not produce the answer. It is not just the religious, but also the more light-hearted young people who know this, in every country imaginable.

What we need is not a new religion but a new culture of morality. We should look more steadily and more sincerely at the morality of the way we treat the world around us. We shall have to find a new relationship between ourselves and our neighbours, between ourselves and people who are ethnically and linguistically and religiously different from us.

The simple text is that we need a new *invironment* before we can achieve a harmonious total environment. But this means universal change in our education systems and the values that pervade them. I submit, therefore, that we do not need a new religion. What we do need, instead, is a conscious culture of caring.

The Love of God and the Love of Man

From a letter to Patricia Lacey, England, 1988

I don't know about the love of God; never did. I do
know a great many things which I guess have to do
with the love of Man and this planet. That's the only way
I know how to love the Old Boy – by using my life and
talents in that way. I guess that is why Bapak [Pak
Subuh] said that Varindra means Slave of God. Have you
taken a recent look at Abou Ben Adhem by Leigh Hunt (c
1840)? Do, if you haven't. I think it says something about
both you and me.

Abou Ben Adhem (may his tribe increase!)
Awoke one night from a deep dream of peace,
And saw, within the moonlight in his room,
Making it rich, and like a lily in bloom.
An angel writing in a book of gold:
Exceeding peace had made Ben Adhem bold,
And to the presence in the room he said,
'What writest thou?' – The vision raised its head,
And with a look made of all sweet accord,
Answered, 'The names of those who love the Lord.'
'And is mine one?' said Abou. Replied the angel,
'Nay, not so.' Abou spoke more low,
But cheerily still; and said, 'I pray thee, then,
Write me as one that loves his fellow men.'
The angel wrote, and vanished. The next night
It came again with a great welcoming light,
And showed the names whom love of God had blest.
And lo! Ben Adhem's name led all the rest.

Tarzie's most often told story

In December, 1946, I had the opportunity and great privilege to meet with Mahatma Gandhi. My father-in-law at that time was representing our country in India, and I was to be introduced to the great man at his house. So, with my colonial values I went to a British tailor and got myself a spanking new suit in Royal Air Force blue.

That Sunday morning there was Mahatma Gandhi seated on a rattan settee on the lawn, his cane at his feet by his side. A couple of dozen other visitors were gawking some twenty feet away, for in India distance is a sign of respect. I was taken to meet him. He looked up at this splendid sartorial vision and said, 'Oho, one of our smart southern neighbours!' [Sri Lanka being south-east of India.] I felt distinctly slapped on my face. And he turned, because he could not stand the Westernised Oriental gentleman which he himself had been at one time in his life. The others giggled at my embarrassment because people so often love to giggle at others' discomfort.

Mahatma Gandhi saw all this and took compassion on me. Patting the place next to him, he said, 'Sit down right here.' He wanted to make it up to me. So I sat gingerly, poised at the edge of his chair. And I was thinking, 'How on earth am I going to raise my head again?' But like a smart boy in class who asks an intelligent question to get out of a jam, I produced one. I said, 'Gandhiji, because of your work all of us in Asia are going to be free very soon. If you have one piece of advice to give all of us in Asia what would this be?' He looked around, his face kind of purpling with sadness, reflecting for about twenty seconds, I suppose. Then he looked up again, smiling with that incredible toothless grin of his. He said,

'Reduce your wants and supply your needs. Make no mistake. Our needs make us vulnerable enough. Why increase our vulnerability?'